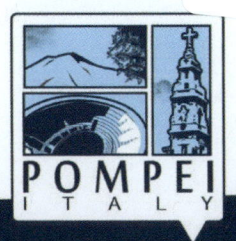

POMPEII
WHAT TO SEE IN ONLY ONE DAY

PRACTICAL TRAVEL GUIDE FOR DIY TRAVELERS

Maria Riatti

Copyright © 2017 **Maria Riatti**

All rights reserved.

ISBN: 1981465677
ISBN-13: 978-1981465675

No part of this document may be reproduced, copied or transmitted in any form without prior written permission of the author.
Except for "fair use" for brief quotations in articles and magazines.

The information in this guide are the result of research and personal experience, then there is no guarantee that they can exactly respond to the needs of the reader or that they are accurate and comprehensive. The author reserves the right to update or change content based on new information. This document is for informational purposes only, in no case shall the author be liable for any problems caused by the use of the information contained in this publication.

If you got a copy of this document from a site that's not www.Pompeiitaly.org or not by the author, then you have a pirated copy.
It took a lot of effort for the realization of this publication, so please help me stop internet crime, report it to the address travelguide@pompeiitaly.org

Write me soon to activate partnerships or collaborations. We want to grow!

www.POMPEIITALY.org

This book was published with
Exclusive Editorial Strategy
"Self Publishing Vincente"
www.SelfPublishingVincente.it

Contents

About me 1
Why to read this guide? 1
How to use this guide book 3
How to get to Pompeii by all means of transport and at all costs! .. 5
How to arrive to Pompeii by Airplane 6
Get to Pompeii by train 7
From Naples to Pompeii by train 8
How to arrive by car 10
Get to Pompeii by other means 12
How to arrive to Pompeii by bus 12
How to arrive to Pompeii by ship 12
On the way to Pompeii 13
Latest advice and maths 13
The best route to visit Pompeii in 2 hours 15
#00 Let's start from Amphitheatre Square 18
#01 Necropolis of Nocera Gate 20
#02 The most majestic monument: the Amphitheatre 21
#03 Carry on with the Large Palaestra 23
#04 Let's speed up and here we are, arrived in Via dell'Abbondanza .. 24
#05 Let's visit the domus of Pompeii 25
#06 And now let's see the productive life with the Fullery of Stephanus .. 28
#07 Among the oldest of the roman world: Stabian Baths 29
#08 The ancient brothel: The Lupanar 30
#09 The Forum of Pompeii, the square where everything happens .. 32

#10 The Basilica is not a church but a tribunal 34

#11 Last step: The Temples 35

We're at the end...or maybe not yet? 36

What to visit after Pompeii if you've half a day free 38

Perfect joint...38

Shrine of Pompeii..40

The Shrine of Our Lady of the Rosary of Pompeii...a bit of history 41

The façade of the Shrine 43

The Picture of the Virgin 45

Discover the ex-voto 48

Do not miss the stunning view from the Bell tower 49

Among the highest towers in Italy...50

Oplontis and the Villa of Poppea 52

Discovering Oplontis..53

Villa of Poppea 54

A walk to Sorrento...56

What to see in Sorrento..57

A dip at the sea..59

The Cove of Mitigliano 60

Wait!! Before you go...62

Credits..66

INTRODUCTION

About me

I come quickly ... my name is Maria Riatti, for more that 3 years I've been writing about Pompeii on the web on my blog Pompeiitaly.org
I live in a town near Pompeii and **I am very familiar with this area**. I love travelling, exploring locations and territories, exploring all what can amaze my eyes, captivate my mind and evoke emotions for my soul.
I work in the web world and I am a freelance consultant in a leading provider company. Responsibilities and tasks leave me little time for leisure and for travelling, but I always get the suitcase ready and as soon as I can I run away for a new adventure. I always plan a new trip in short time and in "do-it-yourself" mode.
Combining my passion for travel and for knowledge, as well as my love for my land, I have become a **TRAVEL LOCAL EXPERT**.
Basically I help travelers to organize and plan their travel experience in Pompeii, Mount Vesuvius and surroundings.

Why to read this guide?

Do you know that Pompeii represents a unique and complete testimony of society and daily life in the ancient world from the age of the Roman Empire?
Nowhere in the world there is a place like this amazing example of historical, cultural and social portrait of such an important stage of human history.
Since 1997 the archaeological area of **Pompeii is Unesco World Heritage site**.

Do you know that the archaeological site of Pompeii covers an area of 66 hectares corresponding to the size of 660 football fields?

To visit all the monuments and to scrutinize the knowledge that the exhibits have handed down **it would take an infinite time**.
Unfortunately Pompeii is often only a short stopping of a trip in southern Italy which involves countless destinations to visit in tight times.

Are you planning a tour to Pompeii for just one day or for a few hours and you don't know which route to choose?
This travel guide **is an indispensable tool for you**.
It will guide you in the best way to visit the ancient city and to don't miss the most important monuments.

How?
In the following pages you will find a practical guide, **a concentration of valuable information to help you plan your visit to Pompeii**, to optimize your time and to be sure to make the right choices that will help you live an extraordinary experience.
I planned for you a route made of 11 stages which crosses the ancient Pompeii and which will allow you to visit the most important monuments in a few hours.
If you have very little time, by following my directions and by taking a moderate pace **you'll complete the tour in about 2 hours**.
I hope, in any case, that you will succeed to enjoy every stage by proceeding on your tour with calm, planning to complete it in half a day at least.

But there is much more in this book.
My aim is to take you by the hand and to accompany you during the discovery of the wonderful beauties of my territory.
I want to be your Local Expert you can trust in order to organize every aspect of your travel.
In addition to the Tour to visit the excavations, you'll find a whole chapter devoted to all the solutions to get to Pompeii with useful information about all means of transport available and the associated costs.
Still, I thought it might be useful to give you suggestions about other places to visit nearby. In the last part of the book I'll give you 3 very interesting solutions for excursions you can plan if you have half a day free.
But this isn't over.

Introduction

In order to thank you for becoming my reader I have saved for you an exclusive **BONUS** that will allow you to obtain more details, precious suggestions, personalized assistance and special agreements with the best restaurants, hotels, touristic guides and much more.
I am talking you about the **POMPEII TOURIST KIT** that you can obtain free of charge by registering online to this address

pompeii.me/touristkit

Summarizing.
Don't you stress with searching on the web the information that are often incomplete and obsolete. If you want to plan a visit to Pompeii and live at the best an extraordinary experience you just have to follow the indications that you will find in this travel guide.
I have written this book for who, like me, organizes travels in little time and for short time, i.e. fast escapes. It's fundamental, in this case, to optimize everything, to well organize the stages, to embed as more visits and excursions as possible in order to not miss the most beautiful and meaningful attractions.
Finally, it is important for you to know that this book is only a small part of a much wider project which became a reference point for many travelers.
I'll reveal in the last pages what benefits are offered to travelers who choose to have free access to the POMPEIITALY Community.

It's time to start our journey.
See you on the other side.

How to use this guide book

Read it for the first time, in one swallow, comfortably sat in front of your pc.
You'll employ no more than 2 hours.
Explore the links that I provide, valid my tips with other research that maybe you have already done. Get a general idea and use this information to plan your trip. A few days before your departure read it again and score the solutions or proposals that best suit your needs. Save the ebook on your smartphone, so that if you will not be able to access the internet you can always consult it offline. When in doubt,

or when you will have to change your plan, you will be able to review it and easily optimize your choices.

Register now on the web site so you can get the TOURIST KIT.
You will receive in your mailbox the Extra contents, including the timetables, the recommended tour map and the handbook that collects the hearth of all you need to know before your visit to Pompeii.

pompeii.me/touristkit

I'll periodically update this guide with the most recent info I got and, going forward, I will also add more chapters by gathering the feedbacks of my readers.
You're invited too! Send me a comment or a review. Your suggestions will be precious in order to make this handbook of travel still more helpful to other travelers.

If you did not find any appropriate responses to your needs or you need more information, you can contact me through my website or social networks.

Have a good journey to Pompeii!

How to get to Pompeii by all means of transport and at all costs!

Pompeii is one of the most loved city of our beautiful Italy, and it's loved by tourists coming from all the world.

In 2016, **3.209.089 tourists visited the Ruins of Pompeii**. They came here to admire the traces of an ancient civilization, to imagine and to dream of an age that has disappeared and to observe the majesty of Mount Vesuvius.

Pompeii rose over 2000 years ago, but its life, as we know, stopped in 79 a.D.

A beautiful and modern civilization inhabited these places, and its tragic end gave us a <u>unique testimony</u> of the ancient world.

To visit the famous Archaeological Site, you must reach the modern city of Pompeii, located in southern Italy, in the province of Naples.

Getting to Pompeii is not hard because it is well connected to the main Italian cities and reachable by most means of transport.

Also getting to Pompeii from abroad is very easy and convenient thanks to the nearby Naples international airport which allows connections with Europe, USA and many other foreign countries.

Here are all the ways to get to Pompeii

- Airplane
- Train
- Car
- Bus
- Ship
- On foot

How to arrive to Pompeii by Airplane

Arriving to Pompeii by plane is the best solution for those who reach it from far away.
The closest airport is the one in Naples: **international airport of Ugo Niutta, Capodichino**. Connected with the main capitals of Europe it has, above all in particular seasons of the year, open drafts also with some Extra-European Countries.

The airport of Naples is a port of call for many companies such as Alitalia or Meridiana, or also some of the most famous low-cost companies like **Easyjet**, **Volotea** and **Ryanair**, moreover there are also charter plans and the seasonal flights.

Capodichino is the largest airport of southern Italy and from here many flights to the main European destinations arrive and leave, beyond those to the United States and sometimes even to Russia.
On your disembark in Naples, I suggest you to stop at the EPT tourist office desk located in the arrivals area and open from 8am to 8pm. Here you can ask for information and advices to continue your visit to Pompeii.
At the airport, you can also find numerous services such as currency exchange, ATM, car rental, bars, restaurants and various shops.

Capodichino International Airport is a modern and comfortable structure that welcomes the tourists in a perfect way, offering excellent connections to the city of Naples and its surroundings.
Every 20 minutes there is a bus leaving from Naples Airport and linking to the city centre, from there you can continue your journey and easily arrive at Pompeii.
Thanks to Alibus, you can reach the Central Station of Napoli Piazza

Garibaldi in 20 minutes in a comfortable and safe bus **at the price of 4 euros**. Right on the same route from the Central Station, you can continue to Molo Beverello, from where you can go for mini-cruises and excursions to islands such as Capri, Ischia or Procida. It is possible to buy the ticket on board without any surcharge.

Also from Naples airport you can take the **S3 bus** to get to the city centre **at a cost of 1,50 euros**.
Unlike the bus, this vehicle takes several stops and has a longer journey time.

Then there is the possibility of **getting to Pompeii directly by taxi**, taking care to choose the white cars with permits and fares well visible. Thanks to some taxi companies it is possible to arrive at the centre of Naples **with about 40 euros** of spending, while for Pompeii the fares are more expensive.

You can also rent a car to get to Pompeii. At Naples Capodichino airport there are the main short-term rental companies as well as you can opt for an NCC service, practically car hire with driver. **Once arrived at the Napoli city Centre, you have to find the best solution to continue to Pompeii.**

**Here are all the possibilities.
Are you ready?**

Get to Pompeii by train

To get to Pompeii by train, in most cases, you must first reach the Naples Central Station and take advantage of a local train.
For example, if you are booking a high-speed train such as the FrecciaRossa Trenitalia or Italo, your trip will end at Naples Central Station.

In any case I advice you to consider whether you come from the North, for example from Rome or Florence, including a train line that will stop in Pompeii. You will have to choose a route that goes to Naples but continues to Calabria for destinations even further south of Campania. With this solution, you can avoid staying in Naples and getting to Pompeii directly by train from your departure city.

If you come from the South, however, most likely the trains to Naples also provide a stop in Pompeii. Remember that Pompeii is located more south of Naples, so in this case you won't need to arrive to Naples but you can stop directly in Pompeii if you are travelling with Trenitalia.

From Naples to Pompeii by train

Once arrived at Naples central station Piazza Garibaldi you have several possibilities to finally get to your destination and start the tour of the Ruins.
In the next few lines I will point out the various choices, but don't worry, at the end of this chapter you will find my precious final advice with a precise indication of the costs needed.

The easiest and safest way to get from Naples to Pompeii by train is to use the **Campania Express** tourist train, a special track connecting Naples, Herculaneum, Oplontis, Pompeii and Sorrento.
This is a latest generation Metrostar carrier, running from April 15 to October 15, with a short and fast route. In Naples, Campania Express only stops in Porta Nolana and Piazza Garibaldi, then it makes stops in Pompeii, Oplonti and Herculaneum Ruins.

In less than 30 minutes you can comfortably reach Pompeii from Naples, the ticket cost is **6 euros for one way or 11 euros return**.
You can check schedules and buy online tickets Campania Express.
The arrival station is Pompei Villa dei Misteri, hence, you will have access to the archaeological site from the entrance of Porta Marina.
For those travelling during less touristic periods, that's in my opinion a very wise choice, this solution is not available.

In addition, from Naples central station you can get to Pompeii by Trenitalia train, the arrival station is close to the Shrine of Our Lady of Pompeii.
Travel time from Naples is less than 50 minutes and the ticket costs about 3 euros.

The most widely used and cheapest train to get to Pompeii is the Circumvesuviana, the local train that connects the vesuvian cities.
From Naples central station, by taking the line "**Napoli - Sorrento**"

you will be allowed to stop in Pompei Scavi, in the same station of the Campania Express, **at the lower price of 3,20 euros for run and with a time of travel of approximately 40 minutes**.
This is the more suggested advice but not the more convenient one.

Now I want to give you a better choice, the best solution.
If you want to arrive at Pompeii from Naples by the Circumvesuviana train, I suggest you to use the Napoli-Poggiomarino line and to stop at Pompei Santuario, where, after the unmissable visit to the Shrine of the Madonna of Pompeii, you will be able to catch up, with a short walk through the new city, the income of Piazza Anfiteatro of the Ruins of Pompeii.

This solution will cost 3,20 euros for the ticket and in 40 minutes you will reach your destination.

Here are the reasons of my advice:

- First of all, this railway line is less frequented by tourists, so less crowded.
  You may consider that during the periods of greater afflux there are thousands of visitors a day arriving to Pompeii by train, crowding and making the travel really uncomfortable.

- The cost of the ticket is nearly the half of the Campania Express one.

- Last, if you start your tour from Piazza Anfiteatro you'll be able to follow the best route if you have few hours and you want to see as much as possible.

The Tour to visit the Ruins of Pompeii, that I will suggest you in next chapter, is the ideal one for those who have little time, in fact it previews a walk of approximately 2 hours.
It starts at the entrance of Piazza Anfiteatro and finishes at the income of Porta Marina.

At the exit, you can take the Circumvesuviana train again, now from the very close station of Pompei Scavi, and carry on with your tour to other destinations.

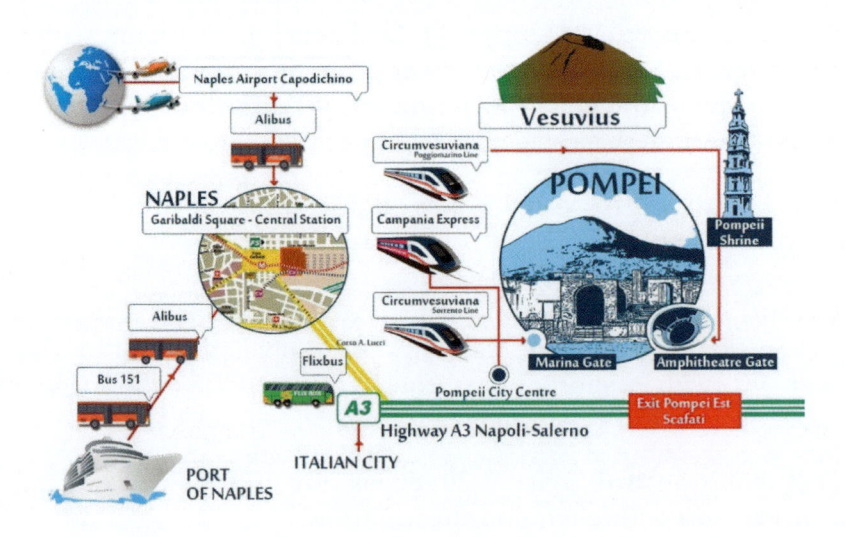

Finally, if your trip solution to Pompeii expected to reach Naples and then continue by train to Pompeii, with a cost of 6,40 euros I would recommend you to use the Circumvesuviana line Napoli-Poggiomarino, Pompei Santuario stop.

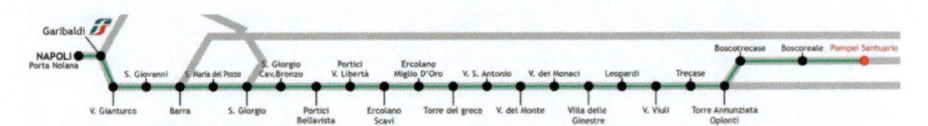

Consider that the visit of the ruins of Pompeii, including the train travel, will take at least 4/5 hours, then consult the timetables of trains to calculate the timing, whereas more or less there is a train every 40 minutes.

How to arrive by car

If you're expected to arrive at Pompeii by car you're in the right section.

The easiest route plans to take the **A3 Napoli-Salerno motorway**, directly connected to the **A1 motorway coming from Rome or from Northern Italy**.
The exit is **Pompei Ovest**. The cost you pay for incoming toll exit in Napoli is **2 euros**. Travel time by car from Naples is around 20

minutes without traffic.
If you come from the South (Salerno), exit at **Pompei Est**, also here the cost of the toll is **2 euros** to be paid in Nocera.

When you arrive in Pompeii with your vehicle, you will need to find a parking spot, choosing between paying public one with blue stripes or a comfortable and secure private parking which is located near the entrance of the archaeological site.

Parking in the blue line along the sidewalks and other areas will cost you **0,50 euros for the first 30 minutes and 2 euros for the next hours**. You must expose the ticket on the dashboard paying in advance at the parking meters located nearby. In order to print the ticket from the parking meters you will need to indicate the number of the parking line on the asphalt where you have parked.
Therefore, when you park, watch the number in the blue line and insert it in parking meter before paying the amount, it only accepts coins in euros.
Obviously, choosing this option for the parking of your car, you will have to preview in advance the break time.

Let me confess you this: I never choose this solution because I personally wouldn't stand the pressure of the deadline of the ticket and the risk to pay a fine.
When on holiday I want to enjoy it without stress!
Don't you agree?

You can then opt for a more convenient solution.
A private parking that previews the payment at the exit, calculating the amount on the base of the hours that you have parked.
At a little walk from Piazza Anfiteatro, there's Piazza Immacolata: here you can find the parking you need!
The cost is of 1,50 euros for one hour and it's for both car and motorcycles.
If you are travelling in caravan or camper you only have the option of the private parking, in this case, the cost is of 2 euros per hour.

Here the address on Google Maps in order to catch up it

pompeii.me/parkingmap

Parkings in the city are safe but I suggest you anyway to **not to leave valuable stuff in your car**.
You can never know 😉

Get to Pompeii by other means

How to arrive to Pompeii by bus

Another way to arrive to Pompeii is to use a convenient bus.
Thanks to the offers of many transport carriers it's really easy to get to Pompeii by bus.
As for example Flixbus offers trips to Pompeii starting from the main Italian cities, and sometimes it's very cheap.

If Flixbus offers the direct route, it is also true that other bus companies offer routes to Naples, but then you can move from there using the means of transport as I suggested in the previous pages.
Another possibility, a quite common one, is to visit Pompeii by a private bus trip. In this case, the bus company will have to pay a tax to enter the city, according to the RTZs.

How to arrive to Pompeii by ship

Naples and Salerno are two of the main cruise ships ports of call in the Mediterranean Sea. Many guests choose to spend a day visiting the ruins or the religious events in the beautiful city of Pompeii.

From Molo Beverello in Naples, as well as from the port of Salerno, it is not difficult to find companies that arrange direct transfers for Pompeii.
Also, just outside the port of Naples you will find the bus that will bring you to the central train station in Piazza Garibaldi.
You can take the **bus 151** that in less than 20 minutes will get you to your destination, or the Alibus leaving from near the maritime station.
Here's a link to download a convenient app where you can view the timetables

pompeii.me/moovit

On the way to Pompeii

It's possible to get to Pompeii by other means, of course!
There's people coming here by caravan, motorbike or bicycle, **on foot**. It's not so weird.
The pilgrimage to Pompeii involves thousands of pilgrims throughout the year.

From Naples and from other cities in Campania, walking for tens of kilometers on foot, the devotees to Our Lady of Pompeii arrive at the most important religious celebrations.
On May, in particular way, on the occasion of the closing of the Marian month, the city roads leading to Pompeii are crowded with flows of pilgrims on their way to the shrine.

Latest advice and maths

If you are wondering what solution to choose from among these that I have suggested, **I will now provide you other suggestions that can help you with your choice**.

To get to Pompeii, from anywhere in the world you arrive, **Naples is the first flag to point on your route**.
The only exception if you arrive from southern Italy by car or by train, it will not be necessary in this case to arrive in Naples, which is further north than Pompeii.
You can book a flight from any Italian city and with a good offer you may pay the return trip less than 100 euros.

Once in Naples I recommend you to move by public transport,
I recommend a good option: Circumvesuviana train, with a little less than 7 euros you have a A/R travel.
I suggest you again **to visit the ruins of Pompeii in the afternoon**, especially during hot weather periods, when walking in the sunshine can be really exhausting.
Of course, you'll have to settle for the short path of 2-3 hours but the colors at sunset are spectacular.

If you travel bringing with you bulky luggage you can leave them at the **luggage storage** of Naples station, it will cost you about 5 euros per suitcase for half a day.

Trolley, backpacks and smaller bags can also be left at the free deposit at the entrance of the archaeological site.
The only disadvantage of this solution is that you have to get in and out of the same door to pick up your luggage and then the path becomes double.

Note that **the entrance cost for the ruins is of 13 euros per person (from Apr.1st 2018 the cost will increase to 15 euros p.p.),** and it is always better to purchase it online to avoid queuing which is often very long.

In conclusion, I do the maths for you. I exclude here the trip to Naples because it would provide too many possibilities.

By public transport you can reach Pompeii ruins **in DIY mode, with about 20 euros per person including transportation and admission ticket**.
This is the cheapest solution.

If you want a more-comfy travel, **if you hate the crowded trains where it is warm and there is no air conditioning**, you can opt for a cab, but consider however it will cost you at least 100 euros.

It would be impossible to offer an ultimate choice.
I don't know your preferences and above all I do not know how your plan of travel is organized but my mission is to help you to explore my territory, so rich of treasures to discover. That's why I'll offer you the possibility to contact me to receive further suggestions ad hoc for your travel.

Contact me at **travelguide@pompeiitaly.org**

As object of the mail write "Maria, I need more suggestions about how to arrive to Pompeii".
This will make me understand that you're a reader of this guide and I'll answer within 24 hours.

BUY YOUR TICKETS ONLINE AND SKIP THE LINE

pompeii.me/buyticket

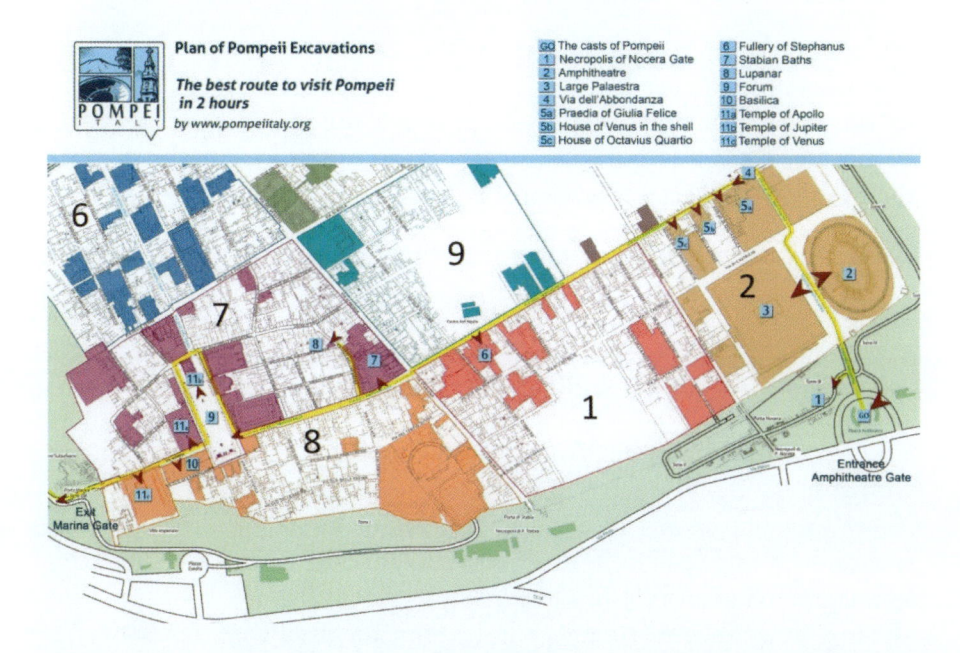

The best route to visit Pompeii in 2 hours

Plan of Pompeii Excavations

The best route to visit Pompeii in 2 hours
by www.pompeiitaly.org

- G0 The casts of Pompeii
- 1 Necropolis of Nocera Gate
- 2 Amphitheatre
- 3 Large Palaestra
- 4 Via dell'Abbondanza
- 5a Praedia of Giulia Felice
- 5b House of Venus in the shell
- 5c House of Octavius Quartio
- 6 Fullery of Stephanus
- 7 Stabian Baths
- 8 Lupanar
- 9 Forum
- 10 Basilica
- 11a Temple of Apollo
- 11b Temple of Jupiter
- 11d Temple of Venus

We've seen all the ways to get to Pompeii, your backpack is ready and now you're arrived at the starting point of the route with your entrance ticket.
You're going to plunge in this exciting adventure and discover all the beauty of this amazing ancient city that was buried by Mount Vesuvius more than 2000 years ago, and finally discovered again thanks to the Archaeological Excavations.
Well...ready?
Follow me, I'll take you into it by the hand.

There are many routes to visit Pompeii, you'll find many of them by reading any guide-book, but the one I'm going to suggest you is the most convenient one if you've just little time to dedicate to it and you don't wanna miss the most important things to see.
Indeed, I planned for you a track that will allow you to cross the whole archaeological site in about 2 hours during which you'll discover all the most important places in town.

It is a journey that you can complete in 2 hours, taking a moderate step but with the chance to stay in the most meaning points, or if you have more time, to enjoy each stage without a hitch.

It's the favorite route chosen by the best tour guides that carry visitors on private tours.
In this regard...if you really want to live a unique and unforgettable adventure, **I suggest you to get a private tour** to enjoy the city. It's the best way to discover it. Oops

Wait... Let's see if I guess what you're thinking at...

"Dear Maria, I'm reading your guidebook because I'm on my way for a free and self-organized tour in Pompeii, then why are you now suggesting me to visit it with a private tour guide?"

You're completely right. You're a self-organized traveler and I agree with you!
There's no better way to discover an unknown country than walking free and getting lost in it, enjoying every hidden corner while trying to imagine what story it has lived.
When you've all your time to enjoy a journey it's always fantastic, but Pompeii is so rich of things to see and places to discover that a whole week wouldn't be enough!
Thanks to a guided tour you can live a short but intense journey catching all the most important cultural, historical and social aspects of the ancient Pompeiians' life.

If that's what you mean, then don't you settle for the first tour you found on the internet or that you'll be suggested at every corner of your track to Pompeii.
You have to choose an authorized tour-guide who's first of all deeply passionate for the archaeological site, who knows any little snippet of the history of Pompeii and who's capable of involving and leading you in this fascinating journey by telling you stories and anecdotes passed on through for more than 2000 years.
I can suggest you some good friends of mine who do this job with passion and enthusiasm and who, besides, were born and grown in Pompeii so they have a deep and inextricable connection with it.
I'll introduce them to you by some interviews I'll post on my blog.

Instead, if the aim of your travel to Pompeii is just to add another "flag" on Tripadvisor, then you can quietly ignore this advice.

The price of the guided-tour is not in your budget?
Don't worry, in this case you just have to follow each step I prepared for you and be ready to catch all the emotions that this place will offer to you.
It may be useful to be prepared for the visit by reading a good book whereby you can study the most important cultural and historical aspect of the city.
But stop chatting... Let's go.

Here the **11 steps tour** for the discovery of the most fascinating places of the Ruins of Pompeii that you'll be allowed to visit in few hours.

But first...
...let's have a peek at the casts of Pompeii.

#00 Let's start from Amphitheatre Square

If you followed my guidelines to get to Pompeii, then you're now at the entrance of Amphitheatre Gate. We're starting from here our tour with an easy route that will allow you to visit the most things with the less time.

From Amphitheatre Gate, you can join different tracks, you can decide to follow step by step every stage of the route I studied for you or you can just leave your inspiration guiding you.
Anyway, you can change at any time your itinerary by making diversions, especially if the long queue at the entrance of the monuments I propose is too long (taking too much time) or if some domus are not opened for the visits in that day.

Are you afraid to get lost?

Take it easy because thanks to the work of the Superintendence it's easy to orient inside the site of Pompeii. You'll just need to follow the signs that are situated at the crossroads.
Did you take the map at the entrance?
It will be very useful!

Moreover, I prepared for you a detailed map of the route I planned.

One of the FAQ on my blog is often: "Where's dead people of Pompeii?"
You've certainly read that **Giuseppe Fioretti**, the most important archeologist who worked at the excavations of Pompeii, gave us the opportunity to discover the human aspect of the tragic pain of the victims of the eruption that destroyed Pompeii, Ercolaneum and Stabiae.

With the technic of the plaster casts he revealed the bodies of the inhabitants of Pompeii, who were found in the same position they had at the moment of the agony that arrived before the end, before they were buried under meters of ash.

In a steel building at the entrance hall, in front of the ticket office, you'll find the casts of Pompeii. Men, women and children crouched and hugged to protect each other from death.
Unfortunately, this building is closed and the 20 casts are now visible only by outside, but a little peek at it will be enough for you to get goose bumps, and you'll understand that it's not art but a terrible reality happened in 79 b.C.

#01 Necropolis of Nocera Gate

You already felt strong emotions, isn't it?
Now cross the entrance gate and start your real journey inside the archaeological site.
Wait a moment...

If you need to use the WC do it now: they are right there, once inside, to the right of the entrance... you'll feel free to start.

The first step will bring you to the necropolis of Nocera Gate.

Once arrived at Amphitheatre Street you'll find on your left a stair that will bring you to an area with not much traffic but actually very important.
The Necropolis of Nocera Gate, that would be the actual "cemetery", owns monuments and buildings that show the funerary architecture of that age.
In particular, there is a building of the Tiberian age, dated between 14 and 37 a.D., built for the family of a priestess of Venus, Eumachia.
Its peculiarity is a high terrace, the esedra, with a burial room and a fence on the back.
This is a beautiful cement work entirely covered by tuff from Nocera

and in the nook, there are nice statues, separated by two semi-columns with a figurative frieze.

You'll be amazed by the sacrality and the silence of this place.

But let's quit talking about dead now.
We're getting straight to the heart of the route now and so we arrive, after few steps from the entrance, at the most impressive building of the Ruins.

#02 The most majestic monument: the Amphitheatre

The Amphitheatre of Pompeii, buried by the eruption of 79 a.D., is the most ancient one of the roman age and it's the most well-preserved in the world.
Built around 70 a.D. it was employed as arena for the circus shows and for the fighting between the gladiators, besides other parades and events.

You can see it all also thanks to the wall paintings and the graffiti found in the place.
In Pompeii there are many wall paintings and graffiti showing these facts.

The Amphitheatre is situated in the south-east part of Pompeii, a suburban area of the ancient city, which in that age was not so crowded and inhabited.

It was the ideal place to accommodate big shows such as the games or the social events dedicated to citizens. Moreover, its building attached to the town-wall made its construction easier.

With a capacity of 20,000 spectators it has been a stage for important events both in Roman times and in today's times.
Does it look little? Sure it is...if we compare it to modern stadiums such as San Siro in Milan that can host more than 80,000 people.

But wait... You must know that Pompeii had about 20,000 inhabitants, while the actual city of Milan has more or less 1,300,000 citizens. It's easy to figure that the Amphitheatre of Pompeii could host the 100% of the inhabitants, while the San Siro stadium can host only the 6,5% of the Milan citizens.

Among the big events hosted in it, I want to remind you that in 1971 the history of rock music has been signed right here thanks to a famous music show: I'm talking about the **"Live at Pompeii"**.
The Pink Floyd recorded here the first part of their movie-concert playing live without audience.

In the area under the stair, a photographic gallery is nowadays set up. It's dedicated to that show and here you can see amazing pics of that historical concert next to the ones of the last one of David Gilmour in the Amphitheatre in 2016. Back in Pompeii after 45 years. This last one has been performed live, for the joy of the fans who crowded the Amphitheatre.

After the gallery you arrive soon in the arena. **Now walk till' its centre. Close your eyes.**

Can you hear the shouting of the crowd, the delirium of the udience? Don't you feel the strength and the tenacity of the gladiators fighting to save their own lives?

#03 Carry on with the Large Palaestra

On the right side of Amphitheatre Square, right in front of the entrance of the Amphitheatre, you can enter into the Large Palaestra, a large, beautiful and fascinating construction.

Built at the beginning of the I century a.D., it was the place dedicated to the training of young Pompeiians. It seems it was built for will of the Emperor Augusto after some new policies of reinforcement of the Empire.
It's a huge square green area surrounded by arcades and in its centre there's a swimming pool large about 800 sqm.
The structure was partially damaged by the earthquake of 62 a.D. and then completely destroyed by the eruption of 79 a.D.
The Palestra Grande is famous for two reasons: inside the area many victims were found: they were escaping from the devastating fury of the volcano; on the columns you can still see many graffiti, left by the writers of that age. One of these, maybe the most famous one, is the **Magic Square**, the most ancient one ever discovered.

Are you guessing what is it and why is it so important?

It's a strange word pun, a composition of 5 palindromes, that's to say

5 words you can read both from right and from left side, and both from the up verse and from down.

It is famous because, during the years, scientists have been trying to give different interpretations, offering hypothesis linked to religion, politic and esotericism.

This mysterious symbol has been found also in other ages after this, and in different parts of the world.

After a restoration lasted 7 years, in 2015 it has been opened again to visitors and now it hosts **the permanent exposition of the findings of Moregine**.

It is not allowed to enter the uncovered area of the Palaestra, but you can only visit it by walking along the lateral arcades.

One of the most loved selfie.
The reinterpretation of the cover of the Beatles' album "Abbey Road", adapted using the pedestrian crossing of Pompeii, is very famous.

#04 Let's speed up and here we are, arrived in Via dell'Abbondanza

The visit of the Amphitheatre, the Large Palaestra and the exhibitions described will take about 30/40 minutes.

Now it's time to proceed quickly along Via dell'Abbondanza.

One of the main streets of Pompeii, the main decuman, is Via dell'Abbondanza, which connects Sarno Gate to the Forum.

Its name has been chosen because of a wrong interpretation of the goddes figurated in a low-relief imprinted in the rock of a fountain situated near the Forum. It's a white fountain picturing a women with big eyes, a

tunic and a cornucopia.
It was confused for the goddess of Abundance, but in fact it is the goddess Concordia Augusta.

This street is very crowded.
Just like at that age was, it is now one of the focus of the city where we see the principal aspects of the daily life of Pompeii and the most important public buildings.
It was the street of the commerce, full of shops and restaurants (pergulae).
Here you'll see, such as in other streets of Pompeii, some big block of rock joining the two sidewalks. These are **the ancient crosswalks** that allowed the passage when the rainwater deluged the streets.
The spaces between the rocks were large enough to permit the passage of the wheeled drays.

#05 Let's visit the domus of Pompeii

The patrician house in the Ancient Pompeii **was called Domus**.
Let's see together its structure.

At the entrance we enter an atrium, a large yard with a pool in the centre which aim was that to collect the rainwater: the **impluvium**. Bedrooms were called **cubicula** and they looked out on the atrium, such as the living rooms and the dining room.

Triclinium is famous: it was the place where they ate and received guests. Its name derives from the three beds on which the commensals layed during the banquets.
Walking through a corridor you arrive at the **peristyle**, an arcade in whose centre you'll see a garden with statues, painted edges and mosaics.
Domus owned by richer people also had a little thermal site.

Now I'll tell you about the first 3 domus that you'll see in Via dell'Abbondanza. I hope you'll be able to visit at least two of them.
All of them are charming, but at the end of this paragraph I'm gonna tell you my favorite one.

Praedia of Giulia Felice

It's one of the most beautiful and large domus of the city, defined "villa urbana"(urban house), it preserves the residue of an orchard and of a garden.
It's 5.800 sqm large and it includes many edifices: a thermal site, a tavern, shops and some apartments surrounded by a big garden.

A wall painting has been found on the frontal wall showing that those apartments were usually rent. In practical terms, the owner, **Giulia Felice**, had good business skill and **created** what we would actually call **B&B with a spa centre** who hosted people looking for wellness and sensorial peace.

The garden is the best part of the building and it has been restored with the original flora.
Roses, ivy and laurel contour the fountain, and vines create a trellis in the oriental side of the garden.
The part of the house where the matrona lived looks like a patrician villa, surrounded by precious statues and paintings now exposed at the Archaeological Museum of Naples.

In 2016 the restoration of the villa ended and it has been opened to

visitors again.
It's part of the route **"Pompei per tutti"**, an itinerary accessible to everyone, also for people with motor disorders.

House of Venus in the shell
Opposite to the entrance, at the bottom of the peristyle, there's a window that seems to look at the sea. **Here you can see the charming painting of Venus**, the patron goddess of Pompeii, lying in a shell while waves move her. With her there are two cupids.
The painting is inspired by Esodo's tale, **"The born of Venus in the shell"**, which tells that the goddess of love was born in the waves of the sea and she was brought to Cyprus by Zephyr. Once there the Ore conducted her to see other Gods.
Venus appears naked, she only wears a diadem in her hair, styled as in Flavious age was, some bracelets and a golden anklet. She has a hand fan. Near Venus there's her lover Mars, painted on a panel aside.

According to researchers, it could be the roman copy of the famous portrait of Campaspe, Alessandro Magno's lover, painted by the most famous artist of that time, Apelle.

It is a beautiful and unfortunate house at the same time, built by an important family of the time, it was damaged by the 62 a.D. eruption. The restoration works started but it was completely destroyed by the eruption of 79 a.D., such as all the population.
Misfortune didn't abandon her even after its excavation: during the second world war in 1943, in fact, it was hit by violent bombardments.
A green garden and many paintings also make this domus wonderful.

House of Octavius Quartio
This house is situated in Via dell'Abbondanza too.
Historical sources affirm that it's the house of Loreius Tiburtinus, and in fact this is confirmed by the wall paintings on its front side.
It's an unusual domus, above all because of all the **elements inspired by the Egyptian** culture, as for example the wall decorations and the marble statues. The garden is charming, full of plants and little pools with water choreographies.

Here you are, the link of an amazing clip in 3D graphic showing the reconstruction of Octavius Quarto's house.

🅿 pompeii.me/octavius-quarto

Here in the Regio II we complete this route and start walking quickly to the Forum.

Oh, wait....I forgot to tell you which domus is my favorite one.
Come on, try to guess...
I'm sure you'd say that's the house of Giulia Felice…instead…

my favorite domus is the last one, the house of Octavio Quartio. And yours?

#06 And now let's see the productive life with the Fullery of Stephanus

Before the eruption of the Vesuvius, life in Pompeii was active, it was an age with many citizens employed in productive works.
In this corner of Campania the job of the laundryman stands out. They were engaged in washing, working and tinging the wool.

In Pompeii you can visit a building called **Fullery, meaning laundry**, owned by Stephanus. We know the name of the owner thanks to a wall inscription.

The Fullery can be compared to a real modern industry: there was, in fact, also a refectory where workers could stay and eat during the work time.
Fulleries were used both to clean the cloths after the operation of filature and tessiture, and for the mere wash of the clothes.

Apart from the impluvium, where big part of the water for the washing process was collected, there are 5 more pools, connected one to each other, and 5 other little pools used to wash again or to tinge the tissues.
Some pestles "kneaded" the cloths with water and soda (*Pompeiians didn't know the soap used in Gallia*) or with human urine.
There were public toilets dedicated to the collection of the urine, called vespasiani, from the name of the emperor who ordered the decree.

Once treated, cloths were washed with chalk or with umbric dust, then pounded and carded.
White clothes or the dyed ones were treated with sulfur to be polished.
The final step was the ironing, made by presses made of stone.
This fullery had also a higher floor with a terrace where they hung laundry.
In the office on the back of the house they found a skeleton with golden and silver coins for a value **of about 10.000 euros**.

I bet you're tired after the visit of the Fullery and you'd like to refresh. Well, on your right you can find the building called "The house of the eagle" where you'll have access to public toilets and meanwhile you'll enjoy a sight from above of the archaeological area.

#07 Among the oldest of the roman world: Stabian Baths

We arrived at the half of our tour, precisely at a crossroad between

Main Decuman and Stabiana Street. Here you'll find **the Stabian Baths (the spa), a public building 3.500 sqm large**.

It's often crowded here so I think you'll have to wait few minutes to access.
From the entrance you'll arrive to a large area formerly used as gymnasium.
Thermal baths during the Roman age were divided in sections, one of them was dedicated to men while the other one to women.
On the right, passing through an arcade, you'll get to the male zone, in the **"apodyterioum"** before (it was a sort of changing room) and then to the **frigidarium**, the bath with cold water. After that you'll arrive to the **tepidarium**, where they had bath in warm water, and in the end to the **calidarium**, hot water.
The heating system of the roman baths was incredibly at the forefront.
There was a plant of tubes in the walls and a floor made with a double stratum system that allowed the cycle of the hot air coming from the furnaces.

Coming back to the yard on the left side of the entrance you'll see the swimming pool.
At the end of the yard, in the north-west side, you'll find the access to the female's zone, smaller and less decorated than the other one.

Here I give you another link of a movie-clip where you can see how baths were made.

pompeii.me/stabianbaths

To continue your route you can exit from the baths by the door facing on Lupanar Street where you'll enjoy the visit of one of the most amazing places in the site.

#08 The ancient brothel: The Lupanar

Roman people loved playfulness, public meetings and liberty.
Lupanar are unusual places, they were the districts of the city dedicated to sexual pleasure, **"red-light quarters"**.

And obviously even in the ancient Pompeii there were whorehouses: a total of 25 brothels was identified in all the city.

Lupanar is one of the most crowded places and you'll probably have to wait for a queue to visit it.
If you are short of time and you're travelling with your family I suggest you to skip this step, besides it's certainly not apt for children.

The story of the lupanar is told by the paintings on its walls.
Here, in facts, there are many **representations of erotic positions**, it's something like an ancient **kamasutra**.
The building consists of 2 floors, the higher one was inhabited by the slaves and the owner.
The lower floor was instead divided into 5 rooms, furnished with stone-made beds, quite little and dark, where Pompeiians could satisfy any erotic desire with the slaves.
You must see also the graffiti indicating the names of the customers, prostitutes or also comments about the sexual positions, and sometimes advices about the sexual diseases diffused.

You certainly know that during the roman age prostitution wasn't illegal, contrariwise they were much involved in searching and promoting activities aimed to satisfy the sexual needs of the citizens, so much so that all **along the streets bringing to the brothel you can see, skillfully carved into the walls or on the floor, representations of phallus** indicating the right direction to arrive there.

You can find further details in this video: "erotic art in Pompeii".

pompeii.me/erotic-art

#09 The Forum of Pompeii, the square where everything happens

Now from the Lupanar go back to Via dell'Abbondanza and quickly reach the end of the road to arrive to the Forum. Here you can finally have a little rest.
I suggest you to have a brief break while you could eat something you brought with you or take nice selfies with the classical "postcard" sight showing the Mount Vesuvius on the background.

The Forum is another essential element of a roman city: a central square, a place where people meet, make business, votes and talks about politics, prays and buys.
It's the real pivot of the community.

It's situated at the crossroad of the main streets of the city. The first entrance, a menacing and huge Vesuvius behind the temple of Jupiter, and on the other side there's the sea. The second one goes to Nocera on one way and to Naples on the other one.

Let's stand in the centre of the Forum of Pompeii, looking at the Temple of Jupiter, and let's try to imagine at how extraordinary could this place be before than the Vesuvius, beautiful but cruel, woke up and destroyed the city.
Here you can see important public buildings such as temples, the Basilica, buildings dedicated to the administration of the city and others destined to the market.

In the centre of the square and near this, monumental works of **Igor Mitoraj** are exposed.
Don't miss the selfie with the sculpture of the **Centaur**, that's by now a real star for tourists.
This bronze work stands in the square and stands out its spear.
The Forum of the Ruins of Pompeii is absolutely one of the most well-preserved Forum above all the Italian ancient cities.

A curiosity to know
When Vesuvius exploded an election campaign was underway. Today you can read on the walls of the city the sponsors dedicated to the electoral campaign: they suggested to vote one campaigner instead of another...but the electoral day never arrived.

#10 The Basilica is not a church but a tribunal

People went to the Forum also to ask for justice, in fact nowadays we still use the word "Foro" to indicate the tribunal (*"for any further controversy" it's written in the contracts we stipulate, "it will be under jurisdiction of the Forum of..."*).

Justice was managed inside the Basilica, situated on the shorter side of the square, in front of the comitium.
The name of this building and the interior look of the room, with columns diving the aisles, remind us to our modern churches.

For Pompeiians - as for all the roman cities - it was different: the basilica was in fact the tribunal, a covered place where the judge gave his judgement after listened the lawyers.

The judge sat on the cathedra at the bottom of the central aisle, where - in our churches - sits the bishop.

#11 Last step: The Temples

How much time has elapsed?
We exceeded our 2 hours, are you tired?
Come on... just a last little effort, we're at the last stage.

Pompeii is a Latin city, its urban architecture is also connected to religion, the ancient pagan one, strongly rooted in the whole Empire.
At the slope of the Vesuvius religious rituals cannot be missed and then the temples make the most of them.
To conclude your visit, stay for a while in one of these wonderful Temples.

The Temple of Apollo, situated on the left side of the Forum.
Dedicated to Apollo, it may be built around the VII century b.C., full of altars, it's a building that could last from the Samnite age.
This is the major religious centre of the city, as many incisions and wall paintings show, or also statues and other findings.

The Temple of Jupiter, on the north side of the Forum.
It's as ancient as the cult of the divinity, it's another pivot of roman culture. In Pompeii this Temple couldn't be missed. It was built, in fact, here in 250 b.C.
It grew during the time and it became always more beautiful, characteristic. It's one of the most particular temples dedicated to Jupiter.

The Temple of Venus, out of the area of the Forum, on Marina Street.
It's a temple you find in any roman city, dedicated to the goddess. It's present in Pompeii to.
It's in a particular position on the top of the valley, it has a charming sight, overlooking the Gulf of Naples. Its story is unusual and complicated.

We're at the end...or maybe not yet?

If you carry on Marina Street, after a steep slope made of pebbles, you'll get to Marina Gate.
If you finished your time dedicated to the visit of the Ruins then use this exit to quit.

I'm sure you followed all the steps I suggested and therefore you're tired.

Do you still have time?

Here a quick list of other stages you can add to your walk in the most famous archaeological site of the world.
- Antiquarium
- Theatres
- Macellum
- House of the Vettii
- House of the Small Fountain
- Villa of the Mysteries

So, your quick but intense visit to the ruins of Pompeii ends here.
Now all you have to do is to buy a souvenir. A book, a souvenir, a gadget to bring to your friends or family: you can easily find it when you exit from Marina Gate

Ahead the exit you can catch the train to come back to Naples...it will be very easy.

WHAT TO VISIT AFTER POMPEII IF YOU'VE HALF A DAY FREE

Hello, welcome back.
Have you concluded your travel through history?

Have you explored the fascinating and mysterious world within the walls of Pompeii?

I'm sure that, although the little time available, these places have transmitted to you memorable emotions and that you are ready to tell them with enthusiasm to your friends.
Hey… if you post a pic on Facebook or Instagram don't you forget to tag me as **#Pompeiitaly**
Every day I share on instagram the nicest photos of the travelers who came to Pompeii and the community of the followers of the account @Pompeiitaly grows every day more… we are over 20.000 people but I am working intensely in order to diffuse the beauties of my territory to a larger audience.

My aim is that to create a Community of Pompeii Ambassadors, join us!

Now your journey continues, later I'll give you some suggestion about how to schedule your time left.

Perfect joint

Before writing this guide I have made a survey among my readers. Among the several questions I made in order to understand the most useful contents I could offer to you, I also asked this:
"How much time you will dedicate to your visit in Pompeii".

The more frequent answer has been:
"1 day".

That didn't sound strange to me.
Pompeii has always been a too much short stage in the plans of the travelers but as I often repeat, it would deserve a depth visit.

As I told you, I am a traveler too and, just like you, **I organize my travels trying to live at the best the destination I choose**. I join as many places as I can visit in order to don't leave anything unseen **and sometimes I get really tired, so tired that I'd need a vacation!** So, I can understand you.

Don't worry, in this section of the book **I'll give you some interesting ideas** about the most interesting things to do here around, if you've scheduled, as big part of the travelers coming to Pompeii, just one day to spend here.

I propose you three routes that include various interests.
The possibilities I'll show you **can perfectly join** the visit at the Archaeological site.
You will be able to choose between these ones following your preferences or just according to the timetable of the Ruins.

If you don't find here the suggestions you were looking for don't hesitate to send me an email at travelguide@pompeiitaly.org

As object of the mail write "Maria, I need more suggestions about Pompeii".
This will make me understand that you're a reader of this guide and **I'll answer within 24 hours.**

3 VISITS IN ADDITION TO POMPEII

- **Shrine of Pompeii**
  For art and faith lovers
  Time needed for the visit: 2 hours
  Don't miss the belvedere from the Bell Tower of the shrine

- **Oplontis**
  For archeology and history lovers
  Time needed for the visit: 2 hours
  Don't you miss the beauty of the garden and the colors of the paintings

- **Sorrento**
  For sea and borough lovers
  Time needed for the visit: 2-4 hours
  Shopping on the main street, Corso, is a must, such as the panoramas of the Communal Villa

SHRINE OF POMPEII

Not only Archaeology in Pompeii
I suggest you to visit it before to start the visit of the Ruins, or maybe in the afternoon to conclude the day. Time needed for the visit: 2 hours

You have followed the travel route that I suggested to you and you arrived in Pompeii by the Circumvesuviana train getting out at the stop Pompei Santuario?

The first stage in the city is the visit of the monumental **Shrine of Our Lady of the Rosary of Pompeii**.
It's situated at 100 m. from the station and it's really easy to get here.
After visiting the Shrine and the bell tower you can proceed to the archaeological site.

Otherwise if you started your visit of the Ruins following the opposite of my indications, then you probably started from Porta Marina and arrived at Porta Anfiteatro. From here you can reach in about 7-8 minutes by walking the city centre, the large and often

crowded Piazza Bartolo Longo, the square in front of the shrine.
You can't miss the visit to the Shrine: you'll need to dedicate to it about 2 hours.
There's no entrance ticket, so it's free.

Once you finish visiting the church **you can enjoy a charming city-sight from the tower bell of Pompeii**.

More than 80 meters high, it allows you to enjoy the wonderful landscape above the city, the view of an extraordinary territory.
It's the perfect place to use as set for a great selfie of your travel here! Don't worry, you don't have to climb the over 300 steps stair, there's a lift that will bring you up there.

Now let's carry on and see an interesting deepening about one of the most important catholic centre of Italy.

The Shrine of Our Lady of the Rosary of Pompeii...a bit of history

The Shrine Our Lady of the Rosary of Pompeii was founded in the late 1800s, right near the Archaeological site of the ancient roman city.
Its history is tied to the figure of a lawyer, **Bartolo Longo**, who was declared blessed in 1980 by Pope John Paul II.

Its construction started **in 1876, on the 8th of May**, with the deposition of the first stone and it has been built thanks to the spontaneous donations coming from faithful from all over the world. It finished on the 7th of May, 1891, with the consecration made by the Cardinal Raffaele Monaco La Valletta.

The Basilica was planned by Antonio Cua, professor at the University of Naples, who designed and directed the building until 1889, when the architect Giovanni Rispoli alternated him.

Originally the shrine had just one Latin cross nave with apse, dome and side chapels and measured 420 sqm.
Subsequently, considered the large flows of pilgrims and faithful, a widening was necessary. It was made between 1934 and 1939, and it brought the Basilica to its actual aspect, with three Latin cross naves and **a surface of 2.000 sqm able to accommodate 6.000 people**.
The Shrine, from its construction till now, survived to many difficulties such as the eruption of the Vesuvius in 1944 and the invasion of the Nazi troops who menaced to destroy it.

The façade of the Shrine

Once arrived at the square behind the building you'll notice **the monumental façade dedicated to universal peace**.

Its construction began in 1894 and it was finally inaugurated on the 5th of May of 1901.
It was designed and projected by the architect Rispoli.
His building was made possible thanks to the contribution of devotees from all over the world who participated in the plebiscite, willed by the founder of Pompeii, as evidenced by the different volumes of signatures preserved in the historical archives "Bartolo Longo".

The façade of the shrine of Pompeii is made of travertine blocks taken from Monte Tifate, in Sant'Angelo in Formis, the same material used to build the Tower of the Church of Santa Chiara in Naples and the Royal Palace of Caserta.
It looks like a church and it's made of two overlapped floors.
In the lower floor, made in ionic order, there are three arcades and ahead there's a large stair which connects the porch to the square.
In the lower part of this first order there's a solid base with four columns made of pink granite from Gravellona, and on both sides you can see four lesenes.
Between the inferior order and the higher one a ledge made of pink granite protrudes, showing the inscription
"VIRGINI SS. ROSARII DICATUM".
The higher floor, in Corinthian order, adopts the same design of the first one.

On the central part there's Pope's lodge. It's adorned with two little pillars showing the emblems of its founders.

On both sides of the big window facing above the lodge there are two columns made of red granite from Finland, with two capitals made of Carrara marble.
On the fronton that closes the central part there's the coat of arms of Pope Leone XIII who declared the Shrine "Pontifical Sanctuary".
On its two sides there are two smaller windows.
The three windows light on a large hall that accommodates **the Historical Archives "Bartolo Longo"**.

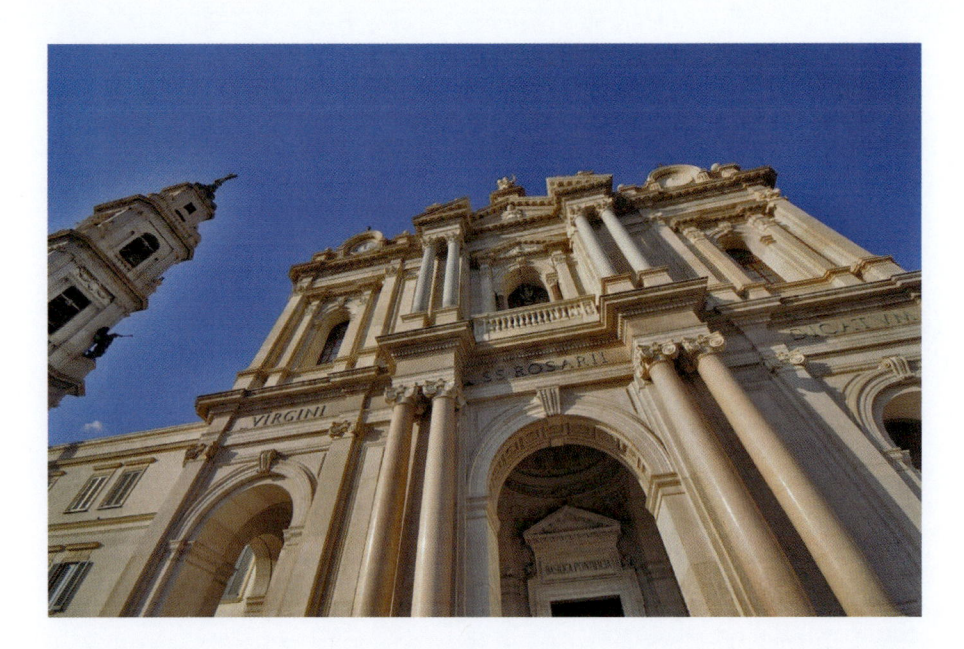

A cornice made of grey granite divides the second order from the attic with a balustrade on which there's **a sculptural masterpiece figuring the Virgin of the Rosary with the holy Child**, a 3,25 meters high statue, realized by the sculptor Gaetano Chiaromonte. He realized it by working on one block of Carrara marble of the weight of 180 quintals.

On the base, that's like a pedestal, **the inscriptions PAX and MCMI**, the year of its inauguration, stand out.

The balustrade is enriched with a dialogic clock and with a meridian one too, fixed up in two decorated rounds, in correspondence of the side windows.

The three entrance doors are decorated with white marble; on the central one there's a pediment and under this there are two cherubim with roses and iris, and the inscription **BASILICA PONTIFICIA**.

The main dome is impressive: adorned with eight couples of granite columns in Corinthian order, eight windows made with colorful windowpanes and festoons.

The higher part is covered with copper with double ribs and at its end there's a granite columns travertine, making the base of the cusp, covered with copper too, with a cross on its top. The dome is surrounded by four smaller domes made with the same structural elements.

The inferior part of the sidewalls of the Basilica is covered with a plinth of red granite from Baveno surrounding the whole structure.
Over the plinth there's a travertine from Tivoli which supports 20 columns made of granite. At the hedge of each columns there's a capital with bas-reliefs and angel heads supporting the cornice above which there's a travertine baluster.

The apses of the side altars are highly relevant.
In particular, on the East side, on the vertical of the dome just **the apse of the chapel of Saint Joseph**, which ends with a pediment on which is carved the coat of arms of Pope Pius XI.
Facing the other side there is the risalit corresponding to the apse of **the chapel of St Michael**, very similar to the other but, ending with a pediment on which is carved the coat of arms of Bartolo Longo.

The Picture of the Virgin

Now it's time to enter the Shrine and let the spirituality of this place pervade you.

Proceed being carefully silent along the side naves, take a look at the frescoes and at the statues, turn a glance up and gaze the majestic frescoes of the central nave.
Ahead you there's the monumental and solemn Main altar, here you can enjoy the view of **one of the most important symbols of faith and devotion: the painting of the Virgin of Pompeii**.

Known all over the world, it attracts millions of pilgrims a year.
The painter of the Virgin of the Rosary is unknown. Let me tell you about the painting arrived here in Pompeii thanks to Bartolo Longo at the end of 1800.

The picture is 120 cm high and 100 cm wide. It represents the Virgin on a throne with the Holy Child on her legs.
Saint Domenico receives by the hands of Jesus the Rosary, while Saint Caterina from Siena receives it from the left hand of the Virgin. Both the Saints are at the foot of the Virgin.
The history of the Picture of the Virgin is connected to that one of the Blessed Bartolo Longo, that, in the attempt to diffuse the practice of the Rosary, went to Naples in order to buy a painting he saw a little time before in a store.

For divine will he met padre Redente, his confessor, who suggested him to go to the Conservatory of the Rosary of Portamedina in his name and to ask to Suor Maria Concetta De Litala **a painting he had given her ten years before**.
Bartolo took his advice but he was deeply surprised when the sister showed him the painting: **a worn and tarnished canvas** with missing pieces of color and with the representation of the Madonna bearing the crown to Santa Rosa instead of Santa Caterina da Siena as in the Dominican tradition.
Bartolo was on the point to refuse the offer, but in the end he decided to withdraw the gift for the insistence of the Nun.

The image of the Madonna reached Pompeii and arrived at the Parish of the SS. Salvatore on the late **13th of November of 1875**, wrapped in a sheet and carried on a cart driven by Angelo Tortora. The cart was used to carry manure.
Who were there when the painting arrived had the same reaction of Bartolo Longo: they remained in dismay. There was also the aged

parish Cirillo.

Therefore, the decision to proceed to the restoration of the picture was taken, even if only partially, because they were afraid that it could be damaged.

The first part of the restauration was made by Guglielmo Galella, a painter who was very popular in Pompeii thanks to his reproductions of the frescoes of the ruins.

Since, later on, the old canvas was further deteriorated, it was restored once again by the Neapolitan painter Federico Maldarelli, who had also care to transform the figure of Saint Rosa in Saint Caterina from Siena.

After that, Francesco Chiariello, another Neapolitan artist, replaced the canvas and stretched it out of few centimeters before the second real restoration was made by Maldarelli.

Another restoration was made in 1965 at the Pontifical Institute of the Order of Our Lady of Mount Olivet in Rome.

This restoration allowed them to discover the original colors of the canvas, which revealed the talent of an artist of the school of Luca Giordano (17th century), and eliminated almost all the gemstones to avoid further damage and punctures to the canvas.

On that occasion, the picture of the Virgin remained exposed for the reverence of the pilgrims for some days in the Basilica of Saint Peter and on the 23rd of April it was crowned by Pope Paul VI.

The return of the Picture of the Madonna of Pompeii was made in a solemn way, with a parade of ecclesiastics and faithful that enlarged as it crossed the cities, along the way from Rome to Pompeii, where the travel ended gloriously.

A last restoration was decided in 2010 by Pope Benedict XVI. So restorers coming from the Vatican Museum started to work on it to eliminate the damages made by the golden and silver clips attached on the canvas as gift for the Virgin.

Pilgrims from all over the world come here to pray the Rosary both on the 8th of May and on the first Sunday of October. They declaim the "Supplica"(a prayer to the Virgin written by the Blessed Bartolo Longo) and pray for God to give peace to the whole world.

Another important celebration, which is very heartfelt by the faithful

of the Virgin of the Rosary, **is the kiss of the picture** that's made every year on the anniversary of its first arrival in Pompeii.
On that day every year the descent of the painting is made, which is placed in front of the presbytery so that the pilgrims can approach and venerate and thank the Virgin with a kiss.

Discover the ex-voto

Every year, millions of pilgrims visit the Shrine, **Temple of the Spirit**, a place of conversion and reconciliation, of mercy and prayer, a safe shelter for the faith.

Even if you are not Catholic, a visit to the Shrine of Pompeii can gift you great emotions for its architectural majesty and its artistic and decorative beauties.

Once exit from the Basilica I suggest you to **visit the gallery of the devotional ex-voto, dedicated to Our Virgin of the Rosary**.
The ex-voto represent the most concrete witness of the faithful who, thanks to the prayer and to the intercession of the Virgin Mary, received graces, overcoming difficult moments and profound suffering.

Entering this place and walking along the corridors on whose walls the numerous ex-voto are exposed, can give you such a deep emotion that you will feel the immense joy and gratitude of those who, with their gifts, have wanted to show and witness the goodness of Our Lady.

Ex-voto are objects, photographs, texts and paintings offered to the Virgin as gratitude for a received grace.

They are not only a testimony of faith, but they represent the perpetual memory of great devotion to the Blessed Virgin Mary and to Bartolo Longo, who listen to prayers and intercede with God.

In fact, offering an ex-voto to Our Lady of Pompeii is only the concluding act of a long and complex process that begins with a request for a divine intervention, continues with the fulfilment of it, then with the pilgrimage to the Blessed Virgin Picture to dissolve from the obligation of the vote and ends with **the show of the gift to make eternal the received grace**.

Do not miss the stunning view from the Bell tower

You can continue your visit of the Shrine by accessing the Museum

where many items coming from around the world are preserved, but **if you have little time, I suggest you go to the top of the Bell tower**.
The ticket costs 2 euros, you can buy it in the shop of religious gifts situated next to the Church.

You can visit the Bell tower **during the spring and the summer, every day from 8.00 to 20.00**, while on Saturday and Sunday it is open until 22,00.
In winter and until the 30th of April the closing time is anticipated to 18,00 during the week days and to 19,00 on Saturday and Sunday.

The last income allowed is 15 minutes before the closing.

The only access for the Bell tower is possible thanks to **a comfortable lift** that will take you to the terrace where you can stop for a short break and enjoy the view.

Among the highest towers in Italy

A breathtaking landscape of the Pompeii Valley, the archaeological site and the Gulf of Naples.
The height of the Bell tower of Pompeii is 82 meters, which makes it one of the highest in Italy, if we except bell towers that are over 90 meters high (in Italy there are 15 in all).

Because of some problems dues to the consistency of the soil it was built on a foundation made with bars of armored concrete pushed deeper than 20 meters.

Designed by Aristide and Pio Leonori, it was inaugurated with a solemn ceremony **on May 24**[th] **of 1925**, in the presence of Bartolo Longo, after 13 years of laying the first stone.
Its structure is divided into three parts:
an exterior part covered with gray granite and white marble, an inside brick made part and a more interior one made of iron to support a staircase of 360 steps and an elevator.

It's in Corinthian style and it is characterized by five overlapping architectural orders, the latter of which has a terrace with balustrade that allows you to admire **the belvedere of the bell tower of**

Pompeii, consisting in the Valley, the Excavations and the Gulf of Naples.

The first order is at the entrance of the tower that is done through a massive bronze door in high relief depicting the scene of the apparition of the sacred heart to St. Margaret Mary Alacoque.
On the pedestals of the third order four great bronze angels are placed.
An electrical system makes the eight bells work. The bells are made of different dimensions and therefore they have different sounds.
The larger bell has a 2 meters diameter and it hungs 50 quintals.

In a niche at the fourth floor there's a statue of the Sacred Heart of Jesus, 5,5 meters high with a weight of 180 quintals, made of Carrara marble.

The Bell tower is crowned with a bronze dome over which there is a cross made of copper and bronze. It's 7 meters high, and it's illuminated during the night so it's visible also at a distance of several kilometers.

The view from the Bell tower is really charming: the whole city is at our foot. Take a look a little ahead and here you'll see the Ruins of Pompeii, an ancient testimony of the splendor of this place.

But the emotions are not over because on the horizon it is possible to notice the Gulf of Naples and on its right lies in its majesty the Vesuvius.

OPLONTIS AND THE VILLA OF POPPEA
SINCE 1997 UNESCO Heritage

I suggest you to visit it before to start the visit of the Ruins, or maybe in the afternoon to conclude the day. Time needed for the visit: 2 hours

To continue your tour in the world of Roman archeology and history I would like to suggest you a jewel that's not much known by the huge tourist influx of these areas: **the archaeological site of Oplontis**, an out-of-the-way route to Pompeii but it's really easy to reach.

To reach Oplontis you just have to reach one **of the three train stations that connect Pompeii, and go towards Torre Annunziata**, the current name of the ancient Oplontis. They are only a few minutes away.
The closest station to the Oplontis excavations is that of the Circumvesuviana train line.

If you are driving from Pompeii just take the A3 / E45 motorway towards Naples and exit at Torre Annunziata Sud.

If there are few hours in the morning, concentrate on the main attractions of Pompeii, and in the early afternoon go to Oplontis, and remember that the **last entry is at 18.00 from April to October and at 15.30 during the winter months**.

Two hours for this visit are enough and even though the train ride is quick you have to consider a total of 3 hours including the trip.

If you combine the visit of Pompeii with the Excavations of Oplontis I suggest you to buy **the cumulative ticket at the cost of 14 euros** - for children it is free.

Thanks to this you'll be allowed to access to 3 archaeological sites for 3 days
(Oplontis, Boscoreale, Pompeii).

You can buy your tickets online, for both the archaeological sites, on Ticketone official website, so you'll avoid the queue at the ticket office. Remember to print it and to take it with you.

Visit this link to buy the tickets:

pompeii.me/ticket3days

Discovering Oplontis

Oplontis is close by the Ruins of Pompeii, its name is the ancient derivation of the current Torre Annunziata, and its archaeological excavations are located right in the centre of the new city.

It was also overwhelmed by the Vesuvius lava during the 79 a.D. eruption.
The first traces of its existence began to spread during the Middle Ages.
Oplontis was designated as a suburban area of Pompeii and a favorite place for rest.

What is to be seen in this small ancient city preserved by the ashes of Mount Vesuvius and arrived till us still intact?

Among the archaeological findings we find: Villa of Poppea; a rustic villa attributed to L. Crassius Tertius, where uncovered bodies involved in daily activities were discovered, and coins in gold and silver too; a spa structure under the current Terme Nunziante.
The only visitable site is the Villa of Poppea, come and discover it.

Villa of Poppea

Built around the 1st century b.C., it is the only visiting monument of the ancient Oplontis.

UNESCO World Heritage Site, it is a residential villa and it was part of the imperial heritage. Both the architecture and the frescoes are in royal style, and they well match with the geometries created by walls and columns.

The western part is visitable, but it has yet to be completely flooded, while the eastern part is already almost completely accessible.

At the moment of the eruption it was being restored and it was uninhabited, perhaps it was damaged by the many earthquakes that characterized the area at that time.
It seems to belong to Poppea Sabina, the second wife of Emperor Nerone.
The beauty of this Villa, besides its exceptional dimension and structural complexity, may be attributed to the presence of **wonderful parietal frescoes** nearly perfectly intact.

You must admire **the Cassata di Oplontis**, a cake painted on the walls of the triclinium that remembers the Sicilian cassata and that was probably made of marzipan and fruit; the famous **basket with the figs**, the golden columns, the amorini, the reproduction of the seasons and a lot more.

A WALK TO SORRENTO

Known all over the world.
I suggest you to visit it in the afternoon or in the evening as conclusion of the day.
Time needed for the visit: 2-4 hours

Not only history but also nature, sea and beauties.
In the Gulf of Naples there are really lots of dream places: Capri rests laid down like a queen in the Tyrrhenian sea with Ischia and Procida.
Then there is Sorrento.
Yes, this time I will escort you to the Sorrento Peninsula, also celebrated by Luciano Pavarotti with the song "Torna a Surriento", in a very special interpretation.

After spending a busy morning in Pompeii, visiting Sorrento can represent the icing on the cake before returning home and definitively conclude your stay in these sun-kissed lands.

To reach Sorrento you can use **the Circumvesuviana train** again,

this time the railway line is **Naples-Sorrento**.
You can take the train from Pompeii by Pompei Scavi station right at the exit of the archaeological site.
If you have adopted my itinerary, you will end up visiting the Excavations at Porta Marina and a few meters away there is the station to reach Sorrento in about **30 minutes**.

Are you here by car?
Then proceed to the SS 145, the entrance is at about 2 km from the archaeological site and it's well marked along the route.
Walking along the coastal road you will be able to admire wonderful views of the Sorrento peninsula and you will arrive at your destination *in about 40 minutes*.

Be aware that in summer it is a very busy road and travel times may be much longer.

Check the traffic conditions before you travel.
It is not advisable to arrive by car in Sorrento on Sunday during summer.

Alternatively, you can also consider hydrofoils by sea. From Naples Central Station, go to Molo Beverello and embark on one of the hydrofoils to Sorrento.
It will be a wonderful experience but you will not be able to schedule it if you have little time.

What to see in Sorrento

Sorrento was built on a ridge of tuff and it is known worldwide for its citrus.
It's one of the most loved place by tourists for its landscapes, that join sea and mountain.
A true place of the spirit and inspiration for painters and writers.

It's told to be anciently connected to Capri by the headland of Punta Campanella.
Many students are actually trying to demonstrate this theory.
Seen from far away the Island Azzurra and Sorrento seem to want to kiss each other.

Your route for visiting the city can begin from **Piazza Tasso**, heart of the historical centre and dedicated to poet of the Jerusalem delivered.
From the arrival station you will reach it in few minutes.

From here you can proceed to Corso Italia, a long shopping boulevard.

Alongside major bookshops, you can find numerous boutiques dedicated to crafts, restaurants and ice-creams.

On one of the sides of Piazza Tasso, take a look at the **Correale Museum of Terranova**.
You know, it accommodates paintings and artworks belonging to a long historical time, from the 16th to the 19th century.

You can admire Italian and foreign porcelain, watches and archaeological findings dating back to the foundation of the city.

Not far from Piazza Tasso you can also enjoy a visit to the **Lignea Tarsia Museum**, inside Pomarici Santomasi Palace.
The building was built in the 18th century and restored in 1999.
Carefully observe its furniture and the wooden objects constructed using the Sorrentino Inlay technique.

This artisan activity is a feature of this place, it was practiced already in the 15th century by the Benedictine monks in the convent of S. Agrippino.

Along the narrow streets of the old town you should stop to buy an inlaid wooden object. A carillon for example. It could be an idea for an original gift, a unique piece.

In the same zone you cannot miss the Communal Villa, you'll enjoy wonderful panoramas.
Your eyes will get lost between the blue of the sea and the sky, interrupted only by the "nearly drowned" shapes of the near islands.

Among the monuments you can't miss there are also **the church of Saint Francesco d'Assisi** with a suggestive eighteenth-century cloister and **the church of St. Antonio, patron of the city**.
Inside this church there's an ancient nativity scene dating back to 1700.

Did you know that the celebrations for St. Anthony fell on February 14?
Correct, **right on Valentine's Day Sorrento is filled with lights, colors and many typical candies** in the place, exposed along the main streets.
One more thing, when walking around Corso Italia do not forget to visit the nearby **San Cesareo lane**.
These little streets are daily crowded by hundreds of tourists, ravished by the typical shops of leather goods and limoncello.

A dip at the sea

Sorrento enjoys numerous beaches suitable for all needs, some of these are equipped with parking.
One of the most striking beaches of Marina Grande is the ancient seaside village. It's of volcanic origin and it has two establishments and a free area where there is no ticket for entry.

You will be amazed by the many colorful houses and boats.
From time to time you will find some fishermen trying to clean the nets or gozzi.
Did you know that for all the world, Gozzi of Sorrento are

synonymous with security and longevity?
These are tiny boats with a tapered shape, with a long sail of 6 to 12 meters.

There is also the beach of Marina Piccola, which can be reached from the centre of Sorrento through the stairs carved into the rock. Even in this case you can choose between free beach and private establishment.

Small advice: stop here to taste some fish entrée in one of the many restaurants in zone.
These restaurants have a beautiful sea sight.
Are you looking for something more intimate?
Here's the right solution for you!

The Cove of Mitigliano

The beach distinguishes from the others for pebbles and particularly crystalline waters, if you are also lover of the trekking it's the ideal choice.
It is located on the coast of Massa Lubrense, situated in an inlet encircled from olive grovs and the Mediterranean spot.
While having bath or lying in sunlight you will enjoy the view of the

island of Capri. To reach the bay you will have to take a trail in Termini, along Via Campanella descent to the junction with via Mitigliano.

If you are a diver lover, do not miss the seaside beauty of the seafront in front of Punta Campanella with gorgonias of all kinds, tuna fish and rudderfishes.
Going deeper you will find a yellow sponge rug that hides a myriad of small organisms ready to be discovered.

Dear reader, our tour ends here, you just have to make your choices and prepare for a fantastic travel experience.
Before going away, find out in the following pages the last valuable advice that can make your trip really special.

WAIT!! BEFORE YOU GO...

When I read a book I always skip the final part where one does not find anything helpful but only some "thanks" and many blablabla things of little interest.
For this reason I decided to engage me even more 'till the end in order to offer to you, in the final part, other helpful contents that will keep you glued to read also the last lines of the book.
At least I try, c'mon!

Now what?
First thing, go immediately to withdraw your exclusive BONUS, by accessing the TOURIST KIT.
If you get registered I'll write you during the next days to give you helpful details and I'll share with you many interesting resources that will help you to plan your trip, by adding new solutions for cheaper and easier excursions.
As next step, I want you to dedicate to a beautiful reading in order to deepen your historical acquaintances about the places that you are going to visit.
My advice for you is the book by Alberto Angela "The three days of Pompeii"

Here the Amazon link:

pompeii.me/albertoangelabook

Do you prefer watching some movies about it?
I have prepared for you a list of the best videos on youtube that you will receive by email as a BONUS resource, part of the TOURIST KIT.

Lastly, **I WON'T ABANDON YOU**
Now that you nearly reached the end I couldn't never abandon you this way.
I already know that you have a question to which you didn't find any answer in this book.

Wait!! Before you go...

I promised to help you, here how to ask for it.

Write me your requirement to this mail travelguide@pompeiitaly.org

In the object of the mail write "Maria, this is my need".
It will make me understand that you have a question to which you didn't find any answer in this book and I will make my possible to answer to you within 24 hours.

ONE LAST ADVICE
It may seem silly but it can make a difference for many reasons.
My last advice for you is:
Book a hotel in Pompeii even just for the night before the visit.

Why is this essential?

1) At 9 am after a good breakfast you'll be at a few minutes from the entrance of the archaeological site, saving the time that you would need for the journey to reach the city.
2) You will be free to devote more time to the visit.
3) You'll find short queue at the entrance (if you buy your tickets online, however, you will skip it)
4) You can conclude your visit at lunch time, after a 4 hours tour. You'll avoid the hottest hours. Trust me...temperatures in summer may increase over 40°.
5) You can leave your luggage at the hotel (almost all of them offer this service for free) and enjoy your hike more freely.
6) The cost of the hotels in Pompeii is on average lower than those of Naples and much cheaper than the hotels in Sorrento.

Another solution that you can consider is to stop more than a day in Pompeii in order to visit the surroundings. In fact from here it will be very easy to reach the many wonderful tourist destinations nearby.
Pompeii is the centre of the world!
You don't know what hotel or b&b to choose?

Don't worry, you will receive my advices by email when you register to the Tourist Kit.

pompeii.me/touristkit

To thank you
I can't wait to receive the report of your experience in Pompeii.
In order to thank you for choosing this book and for being arrived till the end I still have **a gift for you** ... the opportunity to actively participate in my project.

How?
In a very simple way...

Tell us about your experience.
I'm creating a travel journal and you can be the protagonist and thus help other travelers.
Doesn't it look great!?
If you will want it, once back at home after your vacation, write a review of your journey, even a short story with the beautiful things that you have seen, the suggestions that you think to have been more useful or the situations you wouldn't suggest.
In conclusion, **all what can be precious information for other travelers**.
Also add some photo, I will be happy to publish it on our channels as instagram.
This small thought can indeed contribute to improve our "tourist system".

In order to reward you for your contribution you will become "**POMPEII AMBASSADOR**" and I will be happy to send you a little gift as memory of this adventure we shared.
But that's a surprise!
You'll receive all the instructions you need to join the adventure by registering at the Tourist Kit.

LATEST HUMBLE PRAYER
As you can imagine, the word of mouth and the sharing are fundamental in order to make this project grow: therefore, I beg you to talk about my book with your friends and with other travelers, share the link of Amazon on your Facebook and Twitter profile, follow me on the Facebook page and on the Instagram channel, donate 10,000 euros/dollars/bitcoin for my project. Just kidding!!

Well, I think I implored enough.

Wait!! Before you go...

Here all the ways to get in touch with me:
The Facebook page where I post current news, contents and info:

pompeii.me/fb

The Messenger chat to contact me:

m.me/pompeiitaly.org

The Instagram account where every day I share, with the community of beyond 20.000 fans, the beautiful photos of Pompeii and surroundings:

pompeii.me/ig

The official website of the Blog POMPEIITALY.org where you can find many deepenings:

pompeii.me/blog

The page where to get the exclusive BONUS

pompeii.me/touristkit

The Paypal Link to finance my project (if you'd like):

paypal.me/pompeiitaly

I think I really wrote everything.
Thanks from the bottom of my heart... I hope to hear from you soon!
Maria
P.S. If you think this project can somehow intertwine with your interests or activities, please contact me for any kind of COLLABORATION.
P.P.S. Now just the boring but necessary thanks. See you soon.

Credits

First of all I thank you, dear reader, for choosing to follow me on this journey. Completing this project has not been easy, I hope my efforts can really help you!

Many have been the precious contributions of friends who aware or without to know it have made this job possible.

Above all my dearest friend, as well as integrating part of the Pompeiitaly.org project, Carla Peluso. She is the one who manages the instagram and facebook profiles, but above all she's the one who supported me more than anyone else during the work in progress.

Thanks to the trusted Eleonora who supports me in the graphic and the creative part of the project, but above all she supports all my ideas, with a "sometimes absurd" veneration.

This book has been translated by the beloved friend Ilaria Filippo: I thank her for her professionalism and accuracy (if you found mistakes you know who to complain to!)

The beautiful photos that enrich this publication are taken by my dear friend and photographer Rosa Camorino (here her instagram profile), only some of them are mine, but they are the worst ones! Also thanks to Valentina who brought us in a laborious tour in the archaeological site in order to collect these pictures.

I also want to thank some friends and coworkers of mine who contributed to the web project, in particular way MariaRosaria, Francesco, Ilaria and Anna who helped me to arise the blog. Fulvio for his wonderful comic strips Pompeii Junior, Antonella who has cured the "Art" section, Marilena and Eleonora for writing great contents, and new-entry Rosa who will sure carry a great value to the project.

I cannot forget to thank the beloved friends of wesuvio.it, Salvatore, Ciro and Vittorio who involved me in exciting plans for the promotion of our territory.

Finally, special thanks to the people who are every day an inspiration for me to grow and to aspire to great results.

With love,
Maria

GOOD BYE

Plan of Pompeii Excavations

The best route to visit Pompeii in 2 hours

by www.pompeiitaly.org

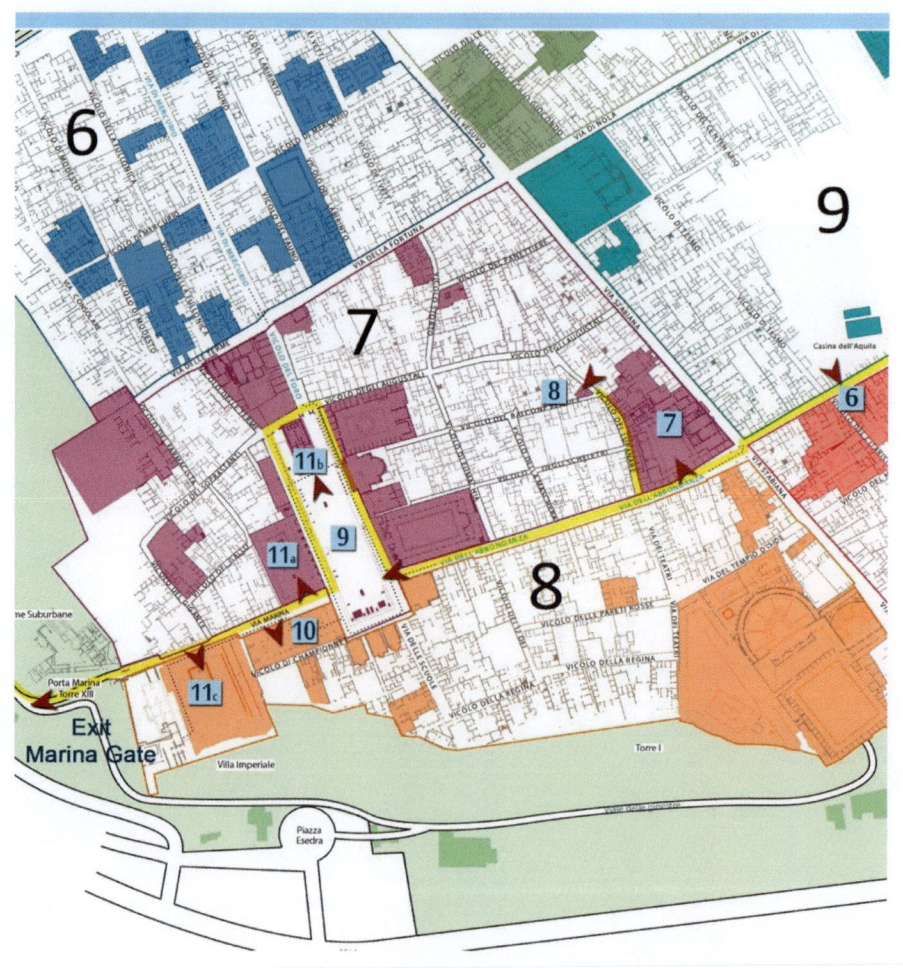

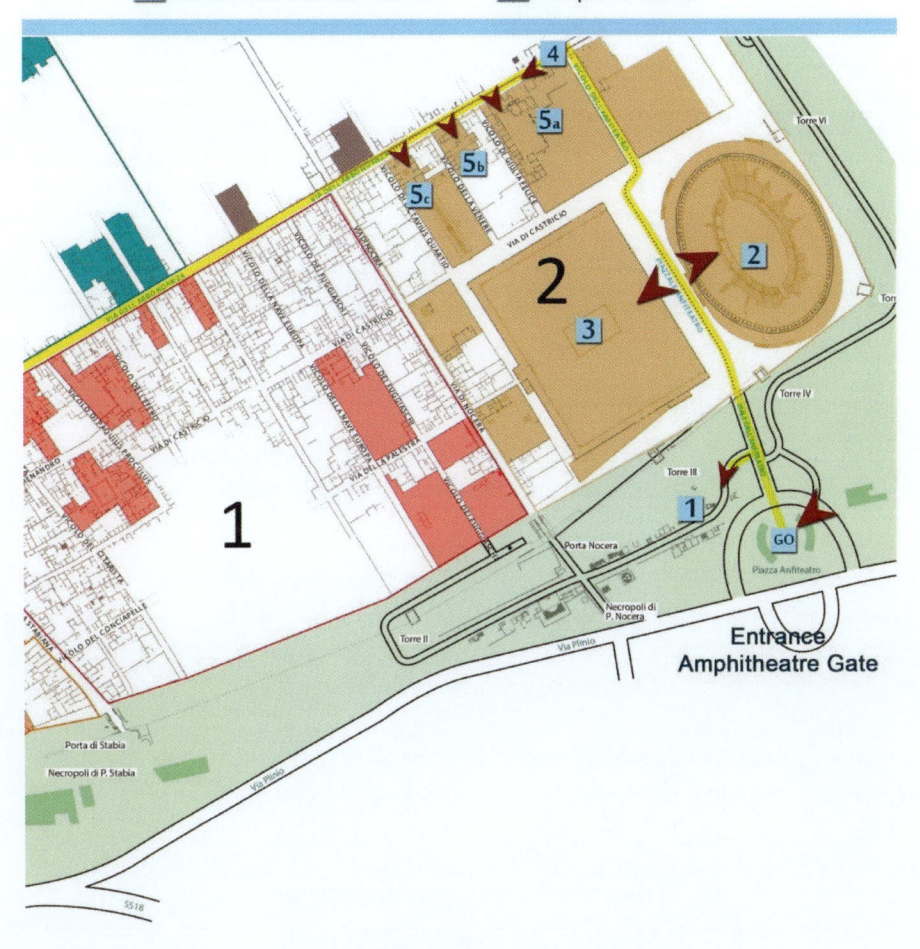

GO	The casts of Pompeii	6	Fullery of Stephanus
1	Necropolis of Nocera Gate	7	Stabian Baths
2	Amphitheatre	8	Lupanar
3	Large Palaestra	9	Forum
4	Via dell'Abbondanza	10	Basilica
5a	Praedia of Giulia Felice	11a	Temple of Apollo
5b	House of Venus in the shell	11b	Temple of Jupiter
5c	House of Octavius Quartio	11c	Temple of Venus

This book was published with
Exclusive Editorial Strategy
"Self Publishing Vincente"
www.SelfPublishingVincente.it

Printed in Great Britain
by Amazon